The Left Behind

The Left Behind

The experiences and challenges of first
generation Black British Caribbean children
left behind in the Caribbean in 1950/60's and
reconnected with parents many years later in
Britain.

First published in 2015
Cover designed by info@geckovisuals.com
Copyright@ 2015 Pauline Dawkins

ISBN - 10:1517723183
ISBN - 13:978-1517723187

In loving memory of my late
mother
ILENE ROSE WILLIAMS
a teacher, nurse, and community
leader
excellent in all her ways. Thank
you for being an
empowering role model mapping a
route for
me to follow that has resulted
in this book

Acknowledgements

I would like to thank my family and friends for coming alongside me
whilst producing this book, and encouraging me all the way, without them
this would have not been possible. Thanking all the contributors, you
know who you are, keep pressing on.   I would specifically like to thank
Bruce for constantly reminding me that I am an overcomer, and dropping a
word at just the right time, for Zoe, Angela, Gail and Hertence for
giving me a shoulder to lean on. Thanking Noel Maclean for being my
watchful supportive shepherd and Sharon's reminder to keep it simple. Jane and Gilda my proof readers of excellence.
Georgina thank you for the blueprint without it this book would
not be here. Maggie thank you for your late in the midnight hour touch, that allowed me to turn the corner on my road to publication. Finally thanking God, who reminded me that I am more than a conqueror.

The Left Behind

CONTENTS
Preface

Left Behind – but moving forward

Preface

This book started out as a series of conversations with family and friends about their experiences as a child, and how this has affected them in adult life.

The book provides insight into the lives of 5 women and 2 men born in the Caribbean, left behind by parents who were economic migrants and who re-connected with their parents, and siblings on arrival in Britain many years later. Their stories may be different to yours but are similar to many experiences I have heard during my formative years with friends and family who were also left behind. Not all experiences were bad, but there were definitely more sad stories than happy ones that led me to write about them. These separations have had lasting effects on our first generation settlers and theirs is a story, that has not really been told, but is often whispered amongst friends, sometimes with tears, sometimes in anger, but always with regret, because this was not the way it was meant to be.

I myself am a first generation British Caribbean child, born in Britain to Jamaican parents who were also economic migrants and came to Britain in the late 1950's. My oldest two sisters were left behind. One joined us around 11 years of age and the other remains in Jamaica to this day. What was the difference between the two? The sister that came here was my mother and father's child, however my oldest sister was my dad's child, born before my parents came together. She remained with her mother and family. Growing up as a first generation British Caribbean child, I always say that I was raised in Britain but lived as a Jamaican child at home, because that was what my parents knew. With time we embraced more and more of the British styles and culture, but my Jamaican heritage was reinforced strongly at home, not just in the food we ate, and the way we lived, but particularly in the stories of Jamaica, that were recited regularly for us to hear. I used to sit on the floor in the sitting room and get excited when my uncles and aunts and their children came to visit because the discussion was all about Jamaica. I sat there visualising what Jamaica, which we called "home", was like: *Ka Ka River*, some way down the gully so that you can't see it from the road with fresh shrimps; Middle hut, the main village shop that sold everything you needed; and old yard, my family's original home and land further into the village. I realised that they still saw Jamaica as home, since they left my sisters in Jamaica because they were planning to return "home", within a year or two after making quick money overseas, in the Mother Country. Most never returned home for many years and others have never been back, a minority has returned to settle as returnees. I still refer to Jamaica as home, because having finally managed to travel there at 21 years of age, I saw why I am the person I am and enjoy the things that I do. To ensure I pass this heritage onto my children, I have until recently travelled "home", every three years so that they don't forget where they have come from, and they stay connected to our family overseas. If my parents had earned good, quick money I would have been born "home" and raised with my other siblings there. But it was not to be.

I can relate to the accounts of others and in particular, comments made by my sister regarding her experiences of leaving Jamaica and her growing up years on arriving in the UK.

Thankfully in comparison with some accounts, I think our family became very close, and spent many a Christmas, Easter and special occasion together, even as adults. However, similar to other accounts, my relationship with my dad for most of my growing up years was a distant one, and was only reconciled in his latter years, and I was born here. Sadly both my parents have passed away and I honestly believe most of my cultural awareness and positivity has come from my mother, who accompanied me on my first trip "home".

But wait this story is not about me, but some of my life experiences are contained in these accounts, so there are many true memories and echoes of time past. People I know have experienced many of these things, things that often cannot be spoken of – due to the offense it may cause. This is a book you need to read if any of what I have written in my preface rings true to you, or has open wounds that you need to deal with. In addition, this preface may have wetted your appetite to understand what others have been through so that we can live together with greater understanding. It's a page turner.

Poem: Abandonment

The Left behind, abandoned, and forgotten,
But only for a season, only for a season,
Isolated, confused and searching,
But there was a reason, there was a reason,
Knowing their place, sticking with their race,
I'll be back, I'll be back, just keep on track.

Tomorrow never came, each day became the same,
Grandpa and grandma, grandpa and grandma,
Aunt's, cousins, family and friends,
But no one ever came, no one ever came,
Yearning for a hug, yearning for that love,
So we learnt to play the game, knowing we were not the same.

Waiting for that barrel, looking for that toy,
Hoping the shoes will fit, hoping it will all fit,
Thinking what do they look like, ma and pa,
How can I connect with them, they live so far,
We're told we're going to England, on a floating bird
I wonder if grandma and pa are coming, I haven't heard.

Leaving granny behind, I'm crying inside
New broom sweep clean, new broom sweep

clean,
New land, new home, new dad, new mum but
no sun,
Who are these siblings, is this how it's done,
Where is the love I so craved for, hugs and kisses
too,
Where is the nurturing, is it not for us too.

School is great, home is sad, why did they bring
me here,
You na turn out good, good fi nutting, good fi
nutting,
Clean , sweep, tidy, keep, get on with their
chores,
Granny please come and get me, get me out this
door,
Please don't leave us gran open up your eyes,
I can't take no more, I'm crying deep inside.

I've made so many friends but home is not for me,
Can't take the abuse anymore, can't take it anymore,
There is hope outside these walls, love lives on,
I'm going to give it a try, I'm here for a reason - but why,
I've got to live for my future, I'm going to learn from my past,
I'm starting a new life, of hope, peace and love, that will last.

Marga lion

My early memories of mum were hazy, like looking through a stained glass mirror; she had me at 15, a young mum, no dad around, with most of my care being provided by my gran and other relatives. I understand mum went away to learn sewing and got pregnant and came back with me. I'm blessed they never named me "dress" because I was the education she came back with. This was not common place but it happened in many a family but conversations were in whispers because mum was not married first.

But mum left me, at a young age, with my aunt to travel to another parish to get work, so my aunt raised me. There weren't other children around, so it was more lonely there. Mum came back for a time and assisted in raising me. Gran then took over when mum and aunt left for England. Funny really it should have been the other way around, but you never questioned things in those days; "Children were definitely seen and not heard". Maybe, because mum was so young she appeared to be in the shadows. My best memory of home was my grand uncle's land, which was so vast that it was like living in a kibbutz. My grand uncle, my grandmothers brother, house was at the front of the yard, his mother in law behind, my auntie behind and we were behind that with gran! My mum got married when I was around four years of age, to my step dad, who I have very fond memories of. It was fun living with my gran, I had happy memories, as I had my cousins to play with and spend time with, up and down road, up and down tree and skylarking, (messing around). Uncle had 5 children around my age and we all grew together, therefore I never missed siblings. Me and my gran uncle's daughters were more like sisters and closer than her real siblings and we got into much mischief together. I can't relate to growing up in hardship, because my gran uncle was not rich but comfortable, as he drove people to town, he ran sound, (Music system) and played out. I remember going over there before the dancing started and we would dance and they gave the little children money. We were well *stush*. I remember my uncle as being a leader and trend-setter as he didn't like to have anything anyone else had got. He always used to be the first one to get things in the village and then when it became popular he got rid of it which is where I think I get it from.

What was home like? Well traditionally each Saturday was beef soup and I never wanted to drink the soup but would eat out the dumplings. I remembered being injured badly once. The pavilion is next to the property where they have show and I cut open my knee trying to crawl under the barbed wire to get into the pavilion. Thankfully it healed without my gran knowing or I would have got beat for being where I should not be. I couldn't help but fass. I can see the Mango tree right now in the front of the yard, dem did call dem mango's beefy because they dem so fat that we had to cut them in half and eat them like grapefruit. Now my cousin's mother was very big and the children had less respect for her because they knew if they are rude she couldn't catch them but she would throw things after them. They usually sold the mango's and we were not allowed to touch them. One day my cousin climbed the tree near our bedroom to get a beefy and fell and cut right through her leg with barbed wire, (yes we never learn, dem call this hard ears, and if you don't hear you will surely feel, and feel she did) and you could see the white within her skin. We strapped it up and no one knew about it til this day, except one of our non pork eating gran's who could not see, hear or walk well and we threatened her with pork soup and she agreed not to tell. Can I remember what bush we used to heal it – no idea, you just knew things in those days but often can't member how you know.

I was left with my gran. I was not hurt or surprised when mum and aunt left me at 9 years of age to go a foreign – to England. I really lived mainly up a top yard, with my gran, uncle and my mischievous cousin/sister. At the time I was an only child but I was to learn much later that I am the eldest of 8 siblings. Well, when mum left, gran had the job to raise me alone. My step dad had already left to do farm work in the states, then went to England and was now sending for my mum.

My God mother taught at the school I attended, so I had some protection. Used to visit godmother a lot. I always wondered why I came to England as I never asked to come and was happy at home but Mum said she got letters to say that I was not being treated well; that's why she sent for me but I can't remember any bad treatment as I gave as good as I got! Dem never mess with me fi long. I was seen as a feisty child, fighting at school and coursing mischief in church, you get the picture. My nickname was Marga lion, marga because I was slim but fierce like a lion and I lived up to it. We got things from abroad but most was way toooo big for me. We used to take the dress bow ties and tie my gran's dress to the chair.

I had no choice. Mum send fi me and I have fi go. When I came to come to England, I was 14 years old. I did not want to come because the Caribbean really was my home, I knew no other. When I arrived I cried for a whole week. I never missed anyone in particular but I missed, "yard", I missed "home".

England was nothing like I imagined, it was dark and gloomy. 1965, Easter, it was freezing cold. When I reached the house I was going to stay in, I thought it was a factory as it was built in red brick, smoke coming out of it joined together, and I was cold, freezing. Most of our houses were separate, detached houses and only factories were linked buildings. What a welcome to Loughborough junction, Brixton. I wished if I promised to behave I could return home but it was not to be for many, many years.

The culture was very different here and I got into trouble as soon as I went to school mainly because I was not understood and I could not talk to my parents so I held it in. I did a reading test to get into school and got put back a year, not because I could not read, but because they did not understand a cultural block that I had, and I could not explain. The book I had to read had the word pussycat in it a number of times, and I would not read it, as pussy was a swear word as far as I knew. School was tough and cruel and unfriendly. Every day I fought at school due to racism, there were 5 blacks in the school in Balham. 2-3 times a week, pupils would walk behind you asking to see your tail, make monkey noise and expression and tell you to go back in your tree and call you jungle bunny. I refused to have lacy up shoes as I always took my shoes off in a fight. I took them off to fight dem wid it.   No one would help you or stick up for you so I always had detention and stood outside in the corridor.   I never used to tell my parents as I wasn't used to having them to talk to so I just dealt with it myself. There was no mobile phone and school texts in those days not like now. Mum really didn't know me and soon after I came to England I asked for some sanitary towels and she shouted at me for knowing about these things. She did not know that I had already seen my period back home. When I asked her for the sanitary towels and she went berserk and asked me what I'm know about sanitary towels. That was within 3 weeks of being in UK and it was off putting, I was supposed to write to her and tell her before I came but we did not have that kind of relationship, so I never told her. Also she did not communicate with me by letter but with the people who had me so I did not know mum enough to confide in her. It was a hard time, when there was no one there I could confide in, being an only child.

I was never sick at "home" but after a year in England I became ill with my stomach, and kept vomiting. She, mum, swear blind I was pregnant and they would not believe otherwise until the doctor said I had gastroenteritis. I was 17 and not pregnant so she assumed I would repeat her error as she was pregnant at 15.   As soon as school years was over I left home. I left school at 16 years on Friday and started work on Monday.

I worked in the boutique in the Strand. Did shorthand and commerce by day release. Came home with my first pay packet, bought clothes and shoes, and mum, hit the roof because I never carried all the money to her, so she could give me a weekly allowance.   I said no. I went out weekends, to the Swan or Ramjam in Stockwell. They both finished at 12.30.

Back in those days I had to have something new every weekend, and I am not having the clothes without the bag and shoes. We lived on the third floor and had to have a wash in the bathroom in the basement. I got dressed to go out, and could not stop for dinner, but at 18 years old, she said "make sure you in by 10".   I came back after it finish at 12.30 went upstairs and my room door was locked, went in my mum's room and saw my key on top of a quarter inch leather strap. She picked up the strap and held it high, and I picked up the chair, then she put down the strap. I realised this would not work and moved out and went to live with friends who was studying nursing in digs at Kings College and stayed there till I found a room in Tooting, then, Balham.

Where was my step father? He was there, and he tried to stick up for me, but she said we always a gang up pan her. He would tell her that he's taking me to the pictures but he took me to a club and picked me up later from the club. I never mind my step father because our relationship was good, he would take me all the way to Kingsway for a concert and go to friend and wait for me to finish to pick me up. She, (mum), never knew.

When I went back to get the rest of my stuff no one was there. I was told mum said she soon come back man. Because of how I left I had to pay for board suddenly, I ended up with a job, and my saving finished quickly as I did not know nutting about signing on.
I got into difficulty as it was near Christmas time, did not want to go home even though they offered and had baked beans and white rice for dinner. They did not know where I lived and they did not ask…….

I left home at 18, got pregnant at 21 and was too scared to tell her I was pregnant.   My son's dad made me tell her.

Now I look back there are certain ways that she still has that means we keep catching up.   She is very negative, always thinks the worst of anything and every situation, judgemental and some old fashioned superstition, and is still trying to treat me like a baby.   Examples of some of her superstitious behaviour is she puts a tape measure on the door to keep evil spirits away, she turns the chair over on the verandah to invite the spirits to sit on the verandah, if you put on your clothes inside out its to do with evil or duppie, when you in a cemetery you not supposed to point finger.

I have come to know her better now but it has taken years. I have noticed mum likes things in small proportions and applies it to everything she does, down to owning little cooking pots. She does not like change, she is a worrier. Before I was saved, (became a Christian), worry would take me over but not now. Mum was not on high earning but used her money well to resettle back home. In these last years we have spent more time together. Mum and step dad used to argue a lot but what I did not understand I do now, he was a large, jovial man that did not let things bother him whereas everything bothered mum.

There were rumours that my paternal dad was in England but I never bothered to look for him, as I had a good step dad and family network in Jamaica. I never asked as I was not concerned. I have not got that bond or urge or love. My aunt finally met someone who knew him, and knew where he was, which led to us meeting up. I met my dad for the first time when I was 30 after I had both my children. I just wanted to see what he looked like and nothing else, more out of curiosity, not excitement.

Was he what I expected? Well we never got on, he was a male chauvinist, drank, gambled and still does but not as much. He is married but treats her badly, including domestic violence, regularly hitting her and drinking. At my 50th birthday party he carried on bad though I did not see it. Me and him catch up because in the height of winter I popped by dad and saw his wife Lynn walking out to get him a paper in the cold while he was in bed. My step dad did not let me go short of love, care; etc. he has now passed away. I was gutted as I was in Jamaica and could not attend his funeral. When my aunt died and she only had 1 years back home I was devastated. I had to forgive my uncle her husband but he was more concerned about his sick sister and therefore delayed my aunt going back home, knowing she only had to 2 years to live, because she had cancer. We think she knew before she left but did not say. I discovered when I met my dad that I am the eldest of 8. One of the brothers died which led to a strain which has not been fully repaired.

I missed home!

Reflections on Marga lion

It takes a village to raise a child, (African term)

Home was lovely but and fun, raised by a community, but missing a mother's contribution. This account paints a thought provoking picture of home with a very young mum, but principally being raised by her grandmother and auntie so that when mum left for work abroad, there was no great loss.

The African term it takes a village to raise a child is exemplified in this case. It is human nature to migrate towards someone who shows you love in order to feel nurtured and grow. Therefore growing up with cousins that to all intent and purposes grew more like siblings temporarily filled the parental gap. Growing up without her dad was not an issue also because her step dad more than compensated for the loss. It clear that where good loving relations are formed early life can be very pleasant. In fact the nurturing of babies by someone other than their mother was a regular expectation with many white Slave owners using the young black mothers to wet nurse their babies. Theoretically speaking apart from giving the baby food I have always felt that other things are passed to the child via breast milk. It is impossible to exactly duplicate the milk, and many pints are consumed by the baby before they begin to walk and understand. If the slave owners understood this they would have done away with wet nursing. The ideal is your biological parents, mum and dad but life has shown me where there is a gap, love can find a way e.g. gran, to fill the gap if you let them.

Fun was making something out of nothing

Upon reflection getting into mischief and having fun was so very different in those days. Mischief was more innocent things like cheekiness and e.g. taking mangoes from the family tree without permission, whereas nowadays to generalise young people's idea of fun is indoors mainly computer games, sports and in extreme cases in gang activities and initiation. Mischief now can involve forms of abuse, violent and unacceptable behaviour, or very minor rudeness. There does not seem to be any middle ground, neutral safe zone, except don't do it.

The pain of separation runs deep
Marga Lion was left behind and wanted to stay left behind and cried for a week. How do we cope with enforced change, do we go with the flow or kick out? Marga lion is successful in her professional and has shown me that sometimes it's better to swim with the tide to survive the wave. If you kick at the wrong time you could drown.

No place to call home
Arriving in England to what looked like rows of factories not homes and a mother that she did not know, and who did not know her was tough. A life that seems nothing like "home", that she cried not for the people but for a place. She left a place of acceptance to a home with stranger parents, and a monster outside the home, called racism. She was being challenged about who she is. It was harsh to feel unwanted and unloved at home and walk to school and feel the same way. Because her mum was a young

mother at the age of 15 there was an assumption that she would not do any better and was constantly put down. She got pregnant at 21, after finishing school, attended evening classes and began working. Talking about feminine things with your mum is an important part of growing up that Marga lion and her mum missed. The compassion and care was not there as all that remained was a physical relationship and love for her mum. "Home" or "backyard" definitely seemed like paradise.

The untrodden road

She was 30 when she met her dad and 7 other siblings. She never missed them but she did miss out on that whole side of her history. It is important to know where you are from. Technically speaking you could end up marrying your own brother just because you don't know what you don't know. The relationship with this side of the family will take time and trust will also take a long time to grow. Life has taught me that one incident can erase bonds of love and trust fused over many years in a moment, let alone new relationship with family members who may not be united themselves. If you are in this situation, don't walk backwards, move forward, learn to trust one experience at a time and put slip ups down to life challenges, we will all have them but every road is there to be walked on, you just need to step out.

Is tradition a hindrance or help?

Superstition is alive and kicking and can be a negative distraction in a relationship, as one is moving forward and the other is stuck in a rut. Drinking bush tea and herbs is ok, but once it stops you doing things like going out you need to evaluate – what do I really believe, and is it a help or a hindrance? Choose to do things in your life that help you and not hinder and encourage others to do the same. You may be the first person to give them a positive steer.

Families need fathers

For me this is an unfinished story. There are raw wounds still bleeding in the family and there is still an opportunity for reconciliation with her father and siblings. The journey may be painful but if this is you it is never too late to build a bridge, families need fathers.

If this account is like looking in the picture of your own history and you would like to paint a fresh one I can suggest possible keys to unlock solutions:

Key 1: Choose to write down what you remember about your own life experience, and how it made you feel and how this has affected you. Who, what and where. Then ask to meet up with the people that have hurt you for tea, and try to talk to them about your past using the notes as your guide. Start by telling them why you are doing this because - you would like to make peace and be re-united.

Key 2: Don't try to remove the hurt and pain of years of neglect and separation in one meeting trust takes time.

Key 3: It's not always about talking, to build relationships, its sometimes about doing, so aim to go out and do something social like bowling, or karaoke to strengthen trust because most of our communication is non verbal, +70%.

Key 4: I would recommend after reading all the life stories that you may need to combine these tips with professional advice. So always consider undergoing a series of professional counselling to talk through any historic concerns that have had a profound effect on your life.

Remember whatever you put off until later is never done - why - because later never comes.

David the soldier

He had a dream.....

I was born in 1960, and though I cannot remember exactly, as I was young, I was left behind around the age of 2, dad left first then mum. Papa and aunt was my mother and father, for so many years. Who was I left with? Well I was left in the care of my mother's father, gran, and their sisters and brother. I was the first child for mum and dad and the only child in the yard. Father's family was up the road, it was a little village in the countryside and in the end I could have been related to everyone in the area. At the time of my birth there were many children in the school that were left behind. It was strange when a white person came to school he seemed to have so much more money. With everything we had, we had to work out how to share. Mandeville and Manchester had a lot of Chinese people. There was some white people in the area, and everyone knew their position. Later on you found that a lot of black men married white women but had to go through the back doors in the hotel up to the 1970's but no one spoke about it. I didn't have to worry about anyone as everyone in the village knew me. We all went to and from school together as a group. On the way home I would cut through my father's mother land and get a dumpling out the pot before cutting through the bush to my home. But even from home there was a rift in the family but as a child I did not know what is was all about but when I left Jamaica older and wiser it had affected me. Anything I got was through my grandfather, who I called papa, mum's dad. With any money they sent I would go and get the slip from the post office and you knew the money was coming from my mum in England and I knew it was for me. We never had gifts at Christmas, nothing special. Except the money and parcels there was no communication with my parents in England, but I did know about them. It was done through papa.

Most things we played with we made it ourselves, catapult or kites but marbles we had to go and buy. We never had much. Saturday and Sunday, when work was finished, we would play cricket with my uncles and we would make the cricket equipment. We had great Easter parade. At Christmas we had Santa Claus and he came on top of the car and was throwing sweets at us.

My grandfather was a preacher so we had to go to church, wherever they saw him, they says they saw me. So Sundays I was with him, going to church in the morning. We would pass three or four churches before I got to the one my grandfather preached at. During the week I leave my shoes off but Sunday's I wore shoes, but not everyone could afford a pair of shoes. My aunt then married and had 2 daughters that I found myself looking after. When did I come to England? I remember it well, it was September 20th 1970 and I was ten years old. I went to town to get my passport and it was amazing looking around at everything. I travelled on my own to England and flew from the capital city, my grandfather and aunt waved me onto the plane. I flew to England on the then BOAC airline that later became better known as British Airways. I remember sitting with 2 other kids, who were brothers and sisters and unaccompanied minors, but I don't know their names because I did not ask. They were eating wotsits and I remembered the girl getting sick. But we never spoke to each other. The hostess came to me and said something, I said yes but I did not understand what she said. We stopped off in America and changed plane, I did not know where I was going but knew to just follow. Having left me so young seeing my mum and dad in England was like seeing them for the first time. I did not know what he looked like but he found me. All I remember my dad saying was "come mi a yu daddy." I was very nervous, and scared but I did not show it. Dad came with a driver. I learnt that they would say dad is a rusty tone man. All I knew when I came here was that I was coming to my mother and father. I never knew about any possible siblings. In the car I was answering my dad's questions and said the customary yes massa, no massa but then dad said lowly and gruffly that there is no massa in here. I never made the connection to slavery days but we were told that's how we were supposed to talk. He shouted at me and I shrunk, it was painful to feel hurt on my first meeting with my dad, where was the love and understanding?

The first person that I saw in the house was my sister, mum was at the hairdressers. After I went in the garden, mum came. I wouldn't say I was happy as everything I knew I left behind and I did not know them. My two brothers who I did not know existed were at school and came home later. They all knew about me but I did not know about them. It's like I was passed on. It like nothing good was expected of me, as there was a lot of name calling that my father did all the time and it was accepted.   The first time went to school at Broadwater Road off, Garratt Lane, my dad said things like "look at you, you imagine the man who came to pick me up can't say I tek you across the road and show him my son." This meant I could not tell anyone from across the road that I was his. I knew I had done nothing wrong but somehow things I did not know were my fault. There was a lot of issues. Once I came over he asked me about his family, and I said to him, I don't know them as I was not living with them. That was like his excuse to have something over me. Years on, he would say he did not want me to stay with my mum's father when I was left behind.   I had to keep quiet as I was respectful and it was not to do with me. Communication was not easy so I never felt able to called my parents, mum and dad, as I did not know them.

Papa died in a car accident, and it affected me really badly, I was not able to eat and kept crying. My dad just told me strongly using swear words to shut up and stop crying. But I was so hurt inside as to me he was my real father, papa had just died as he was the only true dad that I knew.

A year after my dad's mother and father died and I never cried and my father did and mum said I should have cried, but they really did not understand that I never knew them. With my mum she was quietly in the background and did not want to rock the boat, he never hit my mum or was physical in anyway though. Mum took me in the kitchen to help her. I was worried that I would not be able to cook or help as I had been made to feel of no value and replied, "Mi Han no mek Di rice swell. My mum took that as an excuse and said, "When I'm wash it mi no mek it swell, excuse yu a mek." This put me off helping out but mum said don't worry about it, and I still washed the rice and washed up. I always seemed to be doing the washing up and things and they, my brothers get less to do and less hassle. My reading and writing was worse than my siblings, but instead of helping me he shouted so I became more withdrawn.

The only thing my dad did for me was take me down to Balham to get our hair cut, and then further down the road to his sister my Aunt. He only did it the once. Looking back this was a happy moment for me, but was the only thing my dad did with me and I never saw that Aunt again until 1978 or 79. I usually had to take my siblings, my 2 brothers to get their hair cut. We used to walk so that we could buy sweets. Each Christmas some family would be at the house but never that aunt again. My aunt was the sister where mum and dad came to when they first came to England and needed somewhere to live. There was still issues with his sister and my mother, but more to do with the families overseas where it all started. My friends used to see my experience. They used to go cinema with me and my dad would lock me out, yet the others were in the house. My dad used to lock the door when I went out and I had to sleep rough. I was always the scapegoat. When my dad lost £5.00 from his jacket he beat me so bad for it and later when he realised where it was he never apologised. I never had anyone on my side, both were against me in some way. They used to see me on the road but never saw me with anyone, no friends. I was treated like an outcast, my dad would do things with the others and not with me.

I didn't have problems making friends at school etc, but I was scared to go home as I wasn't sure what would happen next. I always get the worst of it but we all got beat. I went to Ernest Bevan school and if I came home late because the teacher asked me to do something he said I need to get a letter as proof but if my brothers came late it was ok. I got what I needed to go to school, clothes etc this was well taken care of. I was 11 and preparing to go to high school and I had to wear a tie. Mum asked me if dad spoke to me, and showed me how to tie my tie. He never did, I had to ask a friends dad to do it but it hurt that my dad never real taught me how to be a man or the manly things that fathers should share with sons. He never really wanted to get to know me, he was very resentful of me. I enjoyed school, and had no problems as I was big enough to defend myself. I dreaded going home though but got through it by keeping quiet. In those days children were seen but not heard.

I was always belittled and when my next brother

in line started school, my dad made it an issue to say that my younger brother was in a higher class than me and started laughing at me. There was no love between me and anyone in the house. 1977 at 15/16 I got a job and they said I must bring my wages home and put it on top of the cupboard and got some back but my siblings never had to do that. I start draw pardner which is a savings scheme between friends, where as long as you promised to pay your regular monthly amount, you could get your money out earlier than you had saved or later. I stopped throwing pardner and because of this my dad told me to leave his house, swearing and shouting at me. I did not understand what I had failed to do, and why he seems to be so angry with me all the time. This was a sad time for me because for a while I was homeless, then mum brought me back home. I did not go to college as I had to earn a living as my dad was not doing nothing for me. I began work as an engineer, which was a good profession and enjoyed playing basketball with my friends, I was very energetic, and sporty.

My father said he is not going to cook for me while my mum and my sister went back to

Jamaica for the first time only my brothers. My dad thought it would bother me, and it has, but I did not let him see that it bother me at the time. I bought special brew and southern comfort told my brothers to put it in the fridge and see what he, my dad would do. For the 6 weeks mum was away he would not touch it, I used the soap powder to wash my clothes as it was sitting there and when my father came back he told me off for using it. I don't talk to my dad and never called him anything, and definitely not dad, and when he died in 2004, I never cried. This left so much unfinished business and unanswered questions, which has gone with him to the grave.

The mistake my mum made with me is by asking me if I still want to look after myself. With dad gone I thought it would be different but as she asked I said yes. We then started having a rift as she continued what my dad had started. When mum was away she saw the drink in the fridge when she came back she asked if she could drink it and I said yes. I believe my dad is lucky that he can only die once.

I realise history really can repeat itself because when I became a father and my daughter was born no one came to see her, or had any interest. The first time they met her she was 8-10 years of age. One time there was a party at our house and none of my friends were invited but they wanted to use my room. My dad came to me later to say it's not him having a party because he knew I was upset. I had a cousin who used to sleep in a shed because of their experience which mirrored mine, but at the time there was no help for me. I suffered in silence.

One day my dad did say to me, " Mi sorry mi run you". I kiss my teeth and walk out.   My dad left me with many questions, why me? I have one beautiful lovely daughter which is a blessing, but we don't cuddle and are not affectionate. Now every Sunday I go to mum's for dinner, collect my containers and come home. Mum calls to ask where am I when I missed coming last Sunday, so the relationship is still not close, but much better. Now he has died, mum is much freer, you can see it.

Whatever is lost, is lost and I can't get it back. But I know the wounds go deep and at times, I can sit and cry at what I have gone through and where I am now. I recently developed a muscular condition that means I am unable to walk far, and it has affected other parts of me. It would have been nice to know what I am inheriting down the family blood line, but with my father gone, the opportunity has been missed and I am left with managing my condition without that insight.

Reflections on David

African sayings
"A tree can never make a forest"

The first thing that hit me about this account is that separation and the legacy of slavery was alive and active when David was growing up and things that other children did not see, he noticed. He may never have commented about this because as he said at the time.

"Everyone knew their place."

Considering the formal end of slavery was in 1834 over 100 years later in the 1950's white children were still treated with exceptional honour because of their colour and nothing else and equality between the races in a black majority country was still lacking. There was progress in that inter marriages were taking place, which were previously not allowed, in fact black slaves were not allowed to marry even their own kind, for 200 years. However mixed couples being treated differently when travelling together was just a reminder that racism was alive and kicking. It must have been soul destroying for a man to have to go in the back door, servants quarters to visit a hotel and his wife enter via the front door. It must also have been demeaning to watch it and accept it. Due to the colour of your skin you were considered worthless. The use of the word massa brought back memories of my dad saying in conversation

Yes, Massa, meaning yes master, but I never made the connection to slavery times until David told me of his experience when using this word with his dad. It was a word I remember being used regularly to mean yes man, or master to someone more senior. As we all embrace change, and develop our identity these words became less said and the history of them forgotten. However it was well known that at that time even in the UK particularly in northern towns pubs segregated black and white customers and American bases for black soldiers was situated away from the army base for white soldiers. Segregation on British soil is not spoken of but was occurring in pockets across the country at the time Caribbean's were being invited to the UK an economic migrant labour force. Trying to grow as a strong, responsible man of authority could not have been easy when you face overt barriers because of the colour of your skin. Thankfully the African saying "It takes a village to raise a children", is so true. And this village spirit enabled David to have a pleasant childhood back home, even though he was aware of family rivalry between him being cared for by his mother's and not father's side.

Communication really is key and it must be so scary arriving in England without any idea what your parents look like but also totally unaware that you had brothers and sisters. You immediately feel you are "an add" on and not fit in. As David's father has died we will never know why he did not want him to come to England and then having paid for him to come, treat him as though he should have never come. Running throughout the accounts are fathers that do not communicate and in this case psychological abuse from arriving in the UK until being run out of the house. Home should be a place of comfort and safety, not pain, fear and sadness. Thankfully he was an engineer, and made something of himself despite the undermining he received constantly as a child. Being the unwanted child does affect the bond you make with others and has clearly affected his relationships, as he is now single, and his relationship with his daughter. We are often a product of what we learn, grow and receive. It is hard to give to others what you have little memory of receiving yourself – love.

If this account brings back pain that has being numbed for so many years I can suggest possible solutions:

Key 1: Write down your thoughts or ask a trusted friend to write them down for you. Carefully reflect on the things from the past and present that are still causing pain in your life. If you are a creative person, use poetry, drawings or whatever means will resonate with you.

Key 2: Try to be open minded as you may be treading on sensitive ground and use the opportunity to talk to other relatives that may be able to tell you about your past so that you can understand your lost parent better, in this case his dad. Use the notes or reflections you have put down to guide your questions. This will also help you understand why your parent responded to you in this way. This may be possible from an aunt or uncle here or by travelling overseas.

Key 3: Choose to forgive them if you can as this will make you feel better. The memories will not necessarily go at all or straight away but over time they will become less painful.

Key 4: Once you are in a better place mentally, it is good to build a bridge. Approach your own offspring by phone or social media first if necessary and then agree to meet up to start the bonding. Then you can deal with your child as history does not have to repeat itself – we do have a choice and our parents choices should not be allowed to affect our children's opportunities, unless we let it.

Key 5: Go away alone or with a friend for a day out if possible to have time to digest everything that has been going on. Spend some time in relaxation to start removing the tension from the past even if this relaxation time is going up 30 minutes earlier to bed so that you can relax and unwind not just sleep.

Key 6: Seek professional counselling if you develop mental health issues as a result of the trauma you have suffered.

Key 7: Keep active and choose to join a club which will redirect your mind and give you the opportunity to make new friends and improve your health and well being.

Remember whatever you put off until tomorrow is never done - why - because tomorrow never comes.

Miss Blossom the bloomer

I never felt like I fitted in

I was born in the Caribbean and came to England when I was 9. They call me Blossom but you know that's not my real name. It's often traditional to be known by one name all your life with only a handful of people knowing your birth name. Why, I will never know. I lived with my siblings three sisters and 1 brother, and I was the youngest.   Therefore I was spoilt because I never got beat, I was sparred. My other siblings got the beating for me even if I did wrong.   I also never liked to share.

Mum left when I was one, my siblings were from three upwards to 6, mum had one child each year. Obviously at that age I had no memory of mum leaving and did not even know what she looked like as I grew. My dad and mum split up after they had my oldest sister but clearly were still trying to make a go of it as they had my other 2 sister, my brother and me. My grandparents raised me. My earliest memory, was of my grandmother showering love on me and her being pregnant and still having children while she was raising us, she had eight.   I was raised with my aunt's and uncle's all living together.

I did not really realise Grandma and grandpa were not my real mum and dad, but though you said these words we meant mum and dad because you never saw your real parents so we never missed them and our grandparents loved me so much I did not feel I had missed out. Every Christmas mum would send down a barrel with toys, sweets, clothes and a hat. I loved it because everything in it was English but I still thought my grandmother was my mother because I was really loved whereas my older brother and sisters did not get as much love so they missed mum and dad more.

I was excited about going to England to see another country and was excited about seeing my younger sister, but not my mum and dad as I did not know who they were, and I already had a mum and dad that raised me. We all flew over together on the BOAC, with my oldest sister and the air hostess looking after us. It was the first time I saw a white woman as the White people in my country were dark, and she had powder on. I was fascinated and kept starring. My parents told us that they were our mummy and daddy and they wanted us to say it straight away. For me that was a personal term and it put me off them and then I began to miss my grandma.

They were not friendly, there was a distance about them. She used to shout all the time and never smiled and was not happy. She treated me like a baby but I wasn't a baby but a little girl now. I think the transition was traumatic for her and us as well. I do call mum, mum now but it took me years. I used to go up to them and tap them in the back and then ask them for something. My dad then noticed and insisted that I call them mum and dad. I did sometimes to please them but was not comfortable. When did I say mum and meant it, around 18 years old, after I left school, 9 years after I first met them. I decided to think about things properly and look more closely at their side of the story, then I chose to forgive.

Though my parents met us at the airport and took us home within 2 years of being in England, my dad moved and began living upstairs. Mum lived downstairs in the same home with us. Dad took over the whole of upstairs, I suppose it was cheaper than going to get two places. Dad did a lot of "sporting", but he never brought another woman in the house.   I used to knock on dad's door to speak to him, it became normality to us. From day one they had broken up but never lived separately until then.

When we had parents evening none of them came.   It's a good job we were great kids and did not get ourselves into trouble.   We did after school activities with the teacher like sports, theatre and opera. We had proper school meals. Really the school took care of us while they were working. They abandoned us back home in Barbados and then abandoned us in England, my oldest sister took the brunt of it washing our clothes, combing our hair.   She was like a young mum, (often called a young carer in these times), looking after her siblings so history was repeating itself. I had a good childhood with the school but we were latch key children, coming into the home with our own keys and looking after ourselves whilst our parents worked. But because there were so many of us we looked after each other. We used to attend the youth club and the guys were into sound system. We spent a lot of time alone in the adventure playground. Our parents did not know we were even there.

I later found out that mum was the oldest of 8 and my mum had to look after them. Dad had 12 siblings, part Indian part black, and he came out dark and African, and was beat because he looked like his father and he was dark. No one taught him how to be a man, he had strong women in his life. That may have been why he hit my mum all the time. Our parents often did not see where we were. My mum was not very affectionate, or hugging because she never experienced this growing up herself, so she did not know how to behave. My dad was never in, very strict and a very horrible christian, very abusive. Kicking mum down the stairs, beating her up and things even when he lived upstairs. After seeing my mum beaten too many times my siblings and I had a meeting and decided to take matters into our own hands, we went upstairs and threw buckets of water over our dad. We expected a beating but was shocked when he called us together to ask us why we did this. I said I had nothing to do with it and said he was a good dad in response to his questions because I was scared but the older ones admitted to doing it. Dad asked if they did not think he was a good dad. They responded and said no as he should not beat their mum. Things changed that day, the beatings stopped, he realised that just providing for them was not enough to qualify as a good dad. He thought as long as he never brought a woman in the house and ensured we had provisions that was all a dad needed to do. I tried to find out why they were like this by asking about their upbringing.

I never knew why but after such a lovely loving upbringing with my grandmother, my own mum treated me so badly. Love with gran, school love but no love at home. She seemed to look down on me and always had something bad to say, if I lost my sock she would say what a stupid girl, she would often say you are going to grow up and have children with many fathers. The saying stick and stones can break your bones but names will never hurt was so untrue, the name calling was really hurting. I was very hurt and was glad that I got solace out of the house at school were I felt loved and in after school care so much so that my time at home was minimal. I tried my best to be away from home as much as possible that even now I enjoy being out of the house more, it has become a habit.

I wondered why mum and dad was like this with me but learnt when I went back to St Lucia and asked questions that my dad never knew love so would find it hard to give love himself. I also learnt that my mum had to delay coming to the UK by a year even though she had the nurses certificate because she fell pregnant with me. As her life with my dad was awful she really wanted to get away. She even tried to abort me by going to a ju ju, (obeah, witch doctor), only the herbs made me stronger in the womb not weaker.   I was therefore meant to be.   I understood the resentment then that my mother had against me and decided to forgive her, as she is just the produce of her own upbringing, and life circumstances.   I decided to forgive, and the relationship has grown ever since. I have since married and have children of my own and shower them with the love I never received. I have tried to ensure they get what I never got, true love.

Reflections on Miss Blossom

I have decided to stick with love, Hate is too great a burden to bear. Martin Luther King

One of the biggest difference that I noticed between the accounts is the difference experiences and outcomes regarding being left behind, based on whether you were left behind alone or with other siblings.

Where Miss Blossom had a good home experience it was clearly due to the fact that her grandmother raised and loved her so much, that even the truth in her life was challenged by her own self. Was grandmother not her real mother? Equally because she had brothers and sisters, and in particular an older sister that took on the role of mother from a young age, she failed to miss her real parents. This would probably not be the same feeling for the older children who had by default to stand into their parents breaches, with no real guide or experience, and yet still learning and growing as a child themselves.

Those of you who know a little about our Black history will know that we are the legacy of many thousands of years of single parenthood and abandonment, principally but not solely during the horrific Transatlantic Slave Trade and for many years thereafter as true freedom was gained slowly over many years post "slavery", e.g. Segregation in Martin Luther King times was only in the 1960's, just the other day, and apartheid ending in South Africa in 1980's. This is just reference to the legalised form of oppression but it is well known that oppression lives on subtly in institutionally racist organisations e.g. Stephen Lawrence enquiry, that need to fight culture's within. This was another example of where the separation has created such a gap emotionally between parents and their sibling that time has had difficulty healing. Resentments from before Blossom was born had affected her and her siblings without their knowledge. History definitely repeating itself with the lack of love from parents because they received little love, no cuddles and hugs. Unfortunately we recreate the past by the negative words spoken into our child unless the children refuse to believe the lie spoken in the heat of the moment. In order to control the slaves they were not only beaten but put down, belittled when spoken to and told they would come to nothing and are nothing. Slaves were not people but commodities and their children had no nurturing and were also commodities, not there to be loved and cherished, but to do things around the home, and mainly on the land. They were not only treated like animals but worse than animals as slave owners treasured their horses more than slaves. Children and adults were owned in slavery days and were dragged up not loved and raised up. Words do have power to hurt and do leave a child wondering what did they do as a child that has caused a parent to resent them so much that they cannot move on. It is easy to develop a complex yourself then as an adult and either struggle to achieve or progress in life or decide and be determined to not let history repeat itself again. Preferential treatment between siblings born here and those born home continued into adulthood however Blossom chose to eventually ignore and accept it and destroy the bitterness that was growing inside her towards her mum due to neglect and her dad due to neglect and domestic violence.

Children witnessing domestic violence is a damaging thing and can lead to feelings of insecurity as an adult and heighten tempers. For a man to hit his wife it is a means of control and manipulation that is wrong. However often men in this situation do not see themselves as behaving inappropriately and consider it to be normal practice, particularly if they saw this as a child or if their friends treated their wives the same way. The child often secretly grow to not just hate what the father does, but hate the father also. Boys fail to learn how to treat girls and girls learn that this is an acceptable way to be treated by a boy. Unfortunately history shows us whether in this country or in the Caribbean that women had little or no rights of their own, and their main purpose was to have children, either to be the breadwinner over in the UK or child slave. Slaves were whipped daily and unfortunately men learnt to beat our women in the same way the slave masters behaved towards us with a clear conscience. Owned not loved. If a slave was seen to do something wrong they would be hit whether or not it was true. Whiping and beating was a form of control to bring about conformity and submissiveness. Nowadays this is less tolerated whether here or in the Caribbean, but it still occurs, secretly and quietly behind closed doors. It's still wrong.

The good news here is that Miss Blossom chose to move on, and chose to love her mum, and get married to a Caribbean man and they have a number of children. Her dad has since passed away without reconciliation. Forgiveness of her mum came with understanding.

Part of the learning often requires you to go back to your mother country and find out why your parents are the way they are. Talk to family members that are willing to talk if your parents won't talk to you so that you can piece together their growing up years which resulted in their adult behaviour. Having learnt that both parents did not experience the hugs and cuddles and love that most children are given now and one child had to be the big sibling and help raise their brothers and sisters whilst their parents worked, was an echo of her experience. Miss Blossom has learnt and has been married for over 25 years with children that you can clearly see are very loved.

Remember whatever you put off until next week is never done - why - because next week never comes.

If this account opens wounds that have never truly healed may I suggest:

Key 1: Reviewing the myth that children are not affected when domestic violence takes place in a home because it is untrue. If you have experienced this you really need to consider if you need professional help particularly if it is still affecting your life and relationships now.

Key 2: Studying the past is an important thing to do, but more helpful if you learn from the past and choose not to imitate the mistakes of old. Ask family and friends about your parents so that you begin to understand why they behave in the way that they do and this may allow you to accept them as they are recognising as with all of us that they have faults. Thankfully we do not always have to be a replica of our parents particular where it results in poor life choices.

Key 3: Start collecting memorabilia's of your parents so that you can remember and reflect on the fond memories as time goes on, rather than live and dwell in the past which may not have been a pleasant experience. Collect pictures and create a photo album especially of your parents and see how many different occasions you can find. This will help to build up good memories that last a lifetime and can be passed on to your siblings breaking the impact of separation.

The Left Behind, the journey and still living in my past

Mum left when I was young, I never missed,
what I never had,
Dad left when I was young, but that was
not so bad,
Granny filled the gap, she cared for me so well,
Siblings and family, and friends galore,
School was fun, learning, games and much more,
I learnt to be disciplined, I walked each day to
school,
With parents overseas, the toys I received were
cool,
We had to do our chores, everyone played their
part,
But later we could play outside, with balls and
stones and kites.

Playing in the yard, finding things to do,
Never a dull moment, everyone around
me I knew,
Getting all dressed up, in my Sunday best,
Going to our local church, this was our day of rest,

Sunday school was fun, the treat was always sweets,
This was definitely my home, this life could not be beat,
Fresh fruit, fresh veg, fresh meat and fish,
no fridge to store food,
But we managed and we grew, and I learnt what I had to do.
Granny I love you so, you always keep me safe,
I am so blessed.

Time waits for no man, I'm growing real fast,
up and up I go,
Families have left for England, a land
I do not know,
I'm told I will be leaving, going on a jet plane,
I'm quite excited, but leaving granny,
nothing will be the same,
I don't want to leave her, but I can't wait to see this land,
I hope it will be fancy, with hot sun, sea and golden sand,
I don't know what mum or dad will be like,
I do want to be loved, treated fair

and well, just right,
I'm off on a new adventure, feel a little scared,
one step at a time.

The plane has many children, travelling
on their own,
I am one of them, as unaccompanied minor,
we are known,
I met mum and dad, other siblings who were
born in England,
They seemed to have so much more than me,
they had a helping hand,
I'm not sure I fit in, can't seem to really bond,
I cry,
My parents try their best, but I miss granny,
I just can't say bye, bye,
I feel like Cinderella, doing so much chores,
and no time for me,
It's cold, and dark here, no fun, no sun, no sand,
no sea,
I have to make the best of it, but where do I
really belong.

I'm trying to say that mysterious word mum,
but I can't,
I'm trying to bond with dad, but he won't,
I learnt to accept I'm different and treated
as such,
But I have risen above it, but sometimes it's
too much,
Picked on at home, dad and mum rowing,
looking for the peace,
Three cannot work, mum and dad split up,
where is the release,
Fragmented as a family, mum here, dad there,
children elsewhere,
Then granny dies and leaves me, life seems
so hard to bear,
I'm taking it in my stride, better days are coming,
but who understands me.

I've finally done it, I've gone and
left the family home,
I feel freedom for the first time,
 I feel fear, I'm alone,
But it's a new adventure,
I really must press on,

I got a really good job, my husband,
my wife won't be long,
Marriage was so quick, I am now divorced,
single and strong,
I have my own children now, for them
I can't go wrong,
It's a second opportunity, to settle here
and grow,
I have my own children now and now there
are things they will never know,
But I choose to keep them close to me,
and do what is right.
I'm going to write my own history,
today, tomorrow, tonight.

Posey Gyal to Cinderella

What age did your parents leave you in Jamaica? Dad left for England before I was born. Mum left early, so I have no remembrance of how old I was when she left. I only remember being raised by my gran and grandad as I was very young. I remember Gran sending pictures of me to England when I was around 2/3 years, so I may have been a baby. It was the done things in those days to leave your children or send them back.

I went to infant school in Jamaica, and primary school in England. I was 7 or 8 and I came over with my sister Monica and my gran on the BOAC plane. It was the first time I went on a plane and I was so excited. I always used to tell my grandad that when I go to England I am not coming back to Jamaica, and I have not been back, but I really miss home sometimes but most of my family are no longer there. Grandad and grandma just thought I was being naughty but I did not like going to the lactrine as I had visions of falling down the hole and it was at the back of the yard, in a hut and I did not like going back there. For that reason and others they used to call me posey gyal, because I was too posh to do mine anywhere. I used to have to empty the possy or potty in the morning that I had used in the night but I never liked going back there. They wanted me to wear yatins which are black material plimsolls, but I wanted my foot to be free and they used to comment that I would not wear yatins. I would wear flip flops if I could not get away with walking with bare feet. I found them very hot. Granny used to say I was cheeky and the name posey gyal stuck.

How did I feel when I left my grandad? Very sad as after a few years he died out there and I could not go to bury him. Gran who came over with us, went to bury him, and I think had gone back a little before he died. Grandad was called papa as he was the only dad I knew in my life and I felt very sad. I was not able to explain why I was so sad and so as not to look like I was taking sides, I kept my sadness to myself. To all intent and purposes my dad had just died and I was inconsolable.

Granny wanted my oldest daughter to come and live with her home but I explained to her that it's different times now and we don't leave our children home. Dad came first to the motherland because they said they needed him, the labour force was low and he would have an opportunity to make his millions, with streets paved with gold, but life was really different. He lived with other people in a shared house, one bedroom, sharing the bathroom and one hob on the fireplace, and then mum came over and lived in one room. When mum and dad had other children they moved to a bigger place with my younger siblings Donovan and Gillian.

My big brothers were the first to leave and came to England. I can't believe I went to England with smoother which is a stocking foot on our heads as granny made us wear it. At the airport I met my mum but I did not know her or my dad. As granny travelled with us we just stuck more with granny as it's who we knew. I then met with my sisters that I didn't know, and to top it all, the weather was awful, it was snowing and cold so mum had coats and hats for us. The snow looked pretty and white but it was too too cold.

Any time I needed things e.g. a new coat, my sisters would say don't go and ask our mum go and ask your mum, meaning granny. We stuck close to granny as this was the only mum we knew. Eventually I had to tell this lady who I should call mother that I need a new coat. Then gran passed away. I was devastated. Gran was buried in Middlesex and we have no idea which one grave it is and we have yet to put on a headstone. I will not feel right about it until this is done.

My sister Monica and I came from a church background and my gran took me to many churches until we ended in a 7th day Adventist so we knew the principles of loving and caring for one another. When we first came here, mum and dad never went to church but eventually they sent us to church. By the time we settled in we were brothers and sisters in primary settings. We hugged and chatted. My brother said he did not want to be here but in Jamaica so he was always running away from home and other things, his coping mechanism to deal with such, a major upheaval in his life.

Who bunks in primary? I did! I bunked off from primary school the odd days because I just did not want to be there and mum and dad never knew. In secondary school I began to see that I am being treated different from the rest.   I felt like Cinderella as I am doing all the work with my sister. Washing a bath full of clothes. Everybody's clothes by hand in a full bath, then ironing between me and my big sister and then mum occasionally helped after work. We used soap powder and soak them in the bath for a time then used a board and the scrubbing brush and the sunlight soap to scrub the clothes including dirty panty, briefs and even snotty handkerchief. Dad did the shopping.   Monica unpack shopping. Rice had to be thrown into something and sifted through. My younger sisters were spoilt and their job was to polish and hoover and they finished quick and we were still working. They were spoil from time. Everybody in holiday time did spring cleaning and chores. I was a rebel from time, only God knows. There was some white girls I needed to beat up because I was being bullied. Why am I being called a bully when I stick up for myself in a predominantly white school where I am being bullied, no one understood, or maybe they just did not care at that time. Everyone was trying to fit in. Mum puts all my **misdemeanours** in her black book in her mind until it overflowed on my bottom. My brother's job was to take out the rubbish as he was never there.

At Christmas I was the one in the kitchen with my mum all hours of night baking with her doing cheese straws and patties when everyone was asleep. When I put the TV on it got hot like fire and so we were told not to put it on, so sometimes when we turned it on without permission we had to turn it off early to cool so that we would not get caught. Dad watched pure news and any kissing programme they turning over the channel over.

In high school later on I bunked more. I did not really make an effort in high school. It's not that I wanted to hang with boys I just wanted a bit more independence which my mum and dad did give me later down the line. I was the first to pay for mum's bill in Wood Green some distance from our house and I was not afraid to learn the bus route and be independent. I used to love it, it made me feel mighty, big and able. One time we went to the park with my brothers and sisters and we were really bouncing my sister on the sea saw and she fell and landed on her front teeth cracking two teeth, her adult teeth needed capping. We got blamed more because we were older.

Mum bought all the drinks at Christmas, me and my older siblings, drank sherry and eventually the sherry got to us. Finally Monica was trying to kill flies with a broom and tried to mash it on the window and lash and broke the window trying to kill the fly. They blamed me as they said I made them do it, I seem to be always accepting the blame.

I wanted to go out on Saturday with my friends to the pictures and I couldn't go but my younger siblings could go for the day to the "library", as their chores were small.

I used to go to the West Indian student centre which is a dance but which was all the way in Earl's Court. We knew people there. If we were going out at 7 daddy wanted us back for 10pm. We used to manage to get back on the last train. One day we came back from Earl's Court in time and decided to go to the party down the road and we walked home with boys. We left the boys part way. The door was locked when we came home and dad opened the door and start lash out on us, and he then let us in and said wait until the morning. We run up to the bedroom before lashes. But usually mum used to do the beating not dad. Mum used to tear down the lashes. One time mum lashed me so hard I ended up in hospital and had to lie and say that it happened another way but because the hospital probed I had to tell them in the end and mum was warned. Did this help? No I got a worse beating when I got home for telling.

When I reached teenager I felt I was grown and needed to trust mum and dad but couldn't. Monica and my two siblings sat and chatted sometimes with mum in the kitchen. I sometimes felt like a loner, I never fitted in. I was a middle child. I never kept a journal except in my mind. I used to stay in my room and plan. A good milestones was my school trips which were always extended so that I could stay out a little bit later, but that was not enough.

Finally I had enough. I just did not fit in and spent so much time alone in our bedroom. One day my sisters went shopping without me. As mum left I phoned a cab, went and told gran I am going shop and took the cab and went. I left home early as I could not take anymore and lived with friends. After a few hours I called gran and said I was not coming back as I couldn't take no more, I was 18.

Reflections on Posey gyal

Be the change you want to see..... Mahatma
Ghandi

Whatever you sweep under the carpet, in your life, is out of sight, but it's still there to trip over, as your own personal mole hill to climb, as a stumbling block. You end up sitting on your issues, trying to ignore it but it still in the way, affecting your life. Tripping through life trying to stand strong but regularly losing your balance. Climbing a hill that has just made your journey of life more tiring and harder. Like a volcano sitting on your issue can be dangerous because there is always going to be a possibility that when things get too hot you explode, and volcanic explosions destroy everything in it's path but does not resolve, as the volcano you sat on remains. What the ash does is cover over the cracks – until the next time. This must have been how poshy gyal felt when she left home, if she did not leave she would have exploded and things would have got much worse, because she had swept her feelings under the carpet.

Not growing up with your mother and father is not too dissimilar from the children that are adopted or fostered in these times because parents and are not able to look after them either because of neglect, abuse or they just did not want the child.

What this discussion showed is that this is where the similarity ends, with distant parents promising to return but never did, yet meagre provisions arrive regularly. But in reality because you are left behind that contradict everything you hear about your parents because what you hear contradicts what you physically see, and you see abandonment. And what is abandonment. It is the act of "surrendering one's claim, right or interest to. In this and other stories it's surrender to other relatives, principally usually grandparents but not exclusively. What makes these experiences so painful is the reconnection in later years, and for some much later years has creating a nurturing gap that is hard to refill as you cannot turn back the past you can only learn from it and try to ensure your future is not a mirror image of your past, as we do tend to recreate and relive our past in our family and siblings inadvertently.

The Cinderella treatment of our Left Behind children is seeing our children as commodities and not their children, to be used as free slaves in the home babysitting for their siblings not dissimilar to the slave days when female slaves wet nursed slave masters babies and acted as babysitters for their children, but though small as it was they were paid. I am not trying to suggest that children should be paid for doing chores in the house but these scenarios echo some of the memories of our past only because the children worked without fair love from their perspective and they could do nothing right but work. Having hard working parents is a good thing but time became the healer so that there is now a proper relationship with her parents. Does she call them mum and dad, sometimes, not very often, and more frequently by their first names, is this because they are not mum and dad? I don't think so but it is a reflection of the way the relationship grew with nurturing beginning too late to catch up with their growing years. Is the relationship perfect – No but there is a love and respect that has come with time, with trust and really because Posey gyal decided to let go of the past, forgive and learn to love again. Sometimes having your own children helps you to see the difficulties that parents do face raising their children and making life changing choices.

If this account has reminded you that it's never too late to rebuild the broken bridges of life I can suggest possible solutions:

Key 1: Decide that you would like to mend the hole in the years of hurt and separation caused by abandonment and loss of belong by choosing to meet with your siblings and try to arrange regular get together so that you can start to rebuild a proper sibling relationship. Try to use common ground, things you all like to bring you together e.g. bowling. Trips to the cinema are not so good as no one can talk to each other.

Key 2: Sometimes meeting up with siblings (particularly the favoured) few can lead to an easier passage to reconnect with your parents as there will be an interest from your parents in how that relationship is developing and the wish not to be left out. Widen the net once the sibling friendship is established to invite your parents along and then make this a quarterly or more often meet up session. Use festive occasions like Christmas and Easter as more people are on holiday from work. Use social media, emails, text and Whats app inbetween but check before you send as short messages can come out harder than intended and offend, less is definitely more though.

Key 3: Try to add the wider family to your gatherings and possible make it an annual family day out so that the next generation feel the love of the family and are not caught up in the issues of the past.

Key 4: Write down all your hurt or put it in a poem if you are creative in that way and give it to your parents after meeting with them or burn it, or rip it up and throw it away, and then choose to move on.

Remember whatever you put off until the future is never done - why - because the future never comes.

Patience the seeker

I was born in Guyana and lived with mum and dad, I knew my dad and got to know him and favoured him before he left to go to England. I was close to my dad because he visited Guyana. I was a pretty child which my dad's friend kept telling me which over time gave me a big head. My earliest memory, was going to school and eating my lunch in the grave yard. I did not have school dinners as gran couldn't afford it, so she met me in the afternoon to bring me my lunch and the graveyard was on the way. That's why I don't like graveyard. Just me and my sister Shirley. I think Joan was too young. Donovan was born in the UK.

I came to England at 7, Shirley 6 and Joan 5 years of age. But before I came to England I had one very bad experience. This has affected my life as a result. I had to go out with my great grandma and we would call her ma, and she used to pinch me but I don't know why. She was very old and died before I left Guyana. I used to hold her hand to help her to the shops because it may have been that she couldn't see. She got knocked over by a car and never recovered. I called grandma granny. To me my granny was like my mum.

I went to school with shoes then later got flip flop, wrote on a slat and later chalk, which we could rub out. School desks were on benches not chairs and we sat straight back. One day I went to a white friends house and I bunked off school and granny met me after school and I got beat with a stick (switch) or belt, I'm unsure which. My chores were to milk the goat while the goat butted me and kill the chicken, and chop it's head off. I used to laugh when they used to run around without any head. I used to play with worms in the dirt but can't stand them now. We had pigs. I remember going swimming in the sea but I'm not sure who took me. We occasionally went to the beach.

What did we do for fun? We would go to church and Sunday school and we went on outings to other churches, beach, and the park. Granny used to make ice cream and I used to help her but I can't remember how to do it now, but remembered us selling it at weddings, functions, and christening. It was lovely.

Then my best friend got knocked over and died. I remember the ice cream van and I have hated funerals ever since. I was about 5 or 6 years old and having an early experience of death. I don't remember her name, and mum was in England by then. Lucy, me and my other friends we may have been related. We saved good clothes for best and played games in our play clothes - we tied rope to tin can and then tied it round our leg, hop scotch and skipping.

Dad did not want us to come over he was having too much fun, but mum saved up and sent for us. We came on flight BOAC and the helper on the plane did not look after us, my sister was sick on the plane and had it down her top. The lady kept and stole our passport and we had to apply for new ones. Our parents came to airport with all their friends. Mini skirt, white plimsolls, short socks, roller neck jumper, cream one side and red the other and she had a bee hive, that's how mum met me. I thought mum looked like a little girl and I think I even asked her why she was dressed like that. When I first saw snow I cried and was walking home from school - to me it was like the sky falling in. No one mentioned it, I did not identify it with reality. I never had a TV as a child so peered through the window and looked at other people's.

The first house we lived in was in Purley. I lived with mum, with 6 families and we all shared a kitchen. The room had a bunk bed, with an alcove for mum and dad's bed and people had to come through our room to use the kitchen. We had paraffin heaters and shared the cooking, women cooked together.   Family and friends were in the same house.

I was excited to go to see mum in England but I cried about missing my gran and when I came over I cried for 6 weeks for her.   I was however close to my dad straight away. Mum was the disciplinarian and around more, she was a nurse. I went to infant school and found that I was ahead as I did joint up writing and they did not do it there. They changed the measurement. As an infant I went through a time of stealing, I used to go into her bag and take her money and did it for a long time until she told me off for it and I cried and stopped. I loved school dinners and even had seconds.   Being with mum and dad was a good memory when I first came here.

My granny died at 93 and I was so upset as I could not return to Guyana to bury her, my maternal mum had gone.

It took long time to bond with mum right up to adulthood, I never used to kiss properly or hug. When did that break, just before dad passed a few years ago. I just took a decision that it's mum, and it happened after my separation and she held me and supported me.

I had my own children that made me happy and I liked seeing my kids enjoying themselves. I became a mother of mother's. Despite the fact that I thought I was adopted because I didn't look like my dad for many years so I asked my mum at 13 and she confirmed I was his but explained that I had another sister though. I behaved differently as I was very very quiet, very shy and very easy to cry and people used to comment that I did not look like them. Did I feel I belonged though? Yes. I found out when I was 13 or 14 that I had another sister. Mum delivered my sister Patricia birthed by another woman, who was her friend, and knew when the baby came out that it was my dad's child. This was taking friendship too far!

Food was the same as in Guyana. First two friends I met were Sonia and Sarah and we stayed friends ever since. I was fascinated by white people and anyone mixed race, fascinated with school as I saw so many white people and loved their ways.   I liked the way they looked not due to wealth and found their food fascinating. I made friends with everyone, including an Asian friends that I used to protect at school as she got picked on so I got invited round her house all the time as her parents loved me for that.

I was not a sickly child and never went to hospital in Guyana or in England as a child. If you had the chance to do it all again would you? No. It was very unsettling, and gave me an unsettled feeling.   What would you have done differently if you could have changed time? I would have been born in England.

Reflections on Patience

Moving Forward – Not Giving up

We must develop and maintain the capacity to forgive. He who is devoid of the power to forgive is devoid of the power to love. There is some good in the worst of us and some evil in the best of us. When we discover this, we are less prone to hate our enemies.
Martin Luther King.

This is the first account with differing experiences about the dead. However it is clear that they held little fear for the things we are often scared of these days like graveyards. However Patience constant eating of her lunch in a graveyard, has rebound with her not liking graveyards and funerals. Some thing's that are strange to us, is a normality elsewhere.
Consider what old experiences you still find is affecting your adult life and consider if it is time to address it, is it time to change the habit of a lifetime and break the hold of your past?

School ways
Now children are forgetting their bags, pencil case, PE kit and lunchbox, we really don't know how good we have it when children had to bring their own chalk, and writing slate,(equivalent now is paper), to school.

Chores
I think more of us would be vegetarians if we had to milk the goat for milk for our breakfast or kill the chicken before we can cook it for dinner particularly as it runs around headless for ages with blood squirting out the top.

Play for one or two

Fun in those days was outdoors, swimming in the sea or river, stepping over a tin can, ice cream outings, skipping, hop scotch, which if brought back would improve relationships between children and youth who seem to spend all their time engaging with computers and not humans.

Church, slavery and segregation

Most activities were centred around the church. This was also the case in medieval Britain with the church positioned in the centre of the village. But for Black Caribbean this was not always the case even up to the turn of the century Black people were not considered acceptable enough to go to white church's as they were just viewed even then as free slaves. Initially when black locals were allowed in they had to sit separately, at the back or attend for a separate service specially for black people. This led as it did in the UK in the early 1950/60's to black people starting up their own church and buying the building of churches that were not being used much. A blessing in disguise.

The trauma of death

My best friend and grandma died. I have to question whether we deal with death and children's experience any different now. I would say no, unless the child demonstrate serious signs of trauma at the time. However for many, the effect comes out in other ways. Often misunderstood over here is the regularity in the early years of this book that accident causing death's occurred. Both had a car accident and died. But to the left behind gran is really mum passing as that was the only real mum they had developed a relationship with. As this can make the biological parents upset these children cannot fully grieve because it will be seen as a sign of betrayal. The loss remains, the pain runs deep and the supportive outlet doors of hope are shut. When I consider the experience of our ancestors in slavery times this was their experience that often slaves were heartlessly killed for very little and thrown in a hole, and everyone had to get back to work. No real time to mourn, and no opportunity to talk through how they are feeling. Unbeknown we can fall into a cycle of historical cultural repetition, because we know our past, (maybe not all of us) but are not learning from our past.

In order to equip future children and support the first generation children we need to be real about our mistakes, as we have all made them, and then embrace change, forgive, live, learn and move on and chose to do better.

Am I adopted

The feelings of separation are compounded if you are the child that looks different. You already have feelings of abandonment being left behind but as infidelity was alive and kicking in those days not being sure if you are a child of your parents may be a real concern because these children struggle to fit in and find their place. A throw back to slavery days is that no one wanted to be different as they would have been picked on by the slave master, and for men, whipped, and for women, abused. They struggle to love because they have already given away that special love to their mother/gran and may think they were left because they were not there parent's child. Whichever way if you are struggling to feel real warm and affection for your parent/s this will be increased by the real feeling that you just don't fit in.

Due to the marginalisation as a child FEAR can control many areas of their lives, but we know that FEAR is False Evidence Appearing Real. So times if you are not sure, you must ask, either a parent or close family member as many a secret has died with the elders that the future generations needed to know, so that we could be empowered or forwarned about life issues we may face.

If this account resonates with you I can suggest a few solutions:

Key 1: Choose to write down what you remember, how it made you feel and how this has affected you. Who, what and where. You must then tear it up and put it in the bin, consciously deciding that the hurt and pain has been transferred to the bin and you are going to live a life now free from any historical pains from the past. If it helps you heal you can repeat this exercise three times to cement your action. In doing this you are choosing to forgive and grow. (I would not suggest more than three times as constantly reading the note can have the opposite effect and bring you down in spirit.

Key 2: Then ask to meet up with the people that have hurt you for tea, and try to talk to them about your past using the notes as your guide and start by telling them that you are doing this because you would like to make peace.

Key 3: Sometimes it's not best to not say all you wish to discuss before you meet as there are wounds open on both sides, so tread carefully and considerately.

Key 4: Always give yourselves a few hours and in a relatively intimate private place, a small cafe for neutrality or yours or their home. Remember if you are at home, or their home and it ends badly it will be harder for you or them to return to visit that home, as there are now more sad memories.

Key 5: Dealing with painful pasts can take time so unless it is one incident you may need to meet up regularly for a period of time dealing with bite size bits.

Key 6: You may wish to go with someone you both trust to start with but remember the relationship you need to repair is with that family or friend not the person accompanying which may hamper discussion as you open up to each other.

Key 7: Try to end each meeting in love, thank them for coming, mention some breakthrough however small that you have both achieved and then agree what you want to address at the next meeting.

Key 8: Regardless of your experience growing up, I'd like to challenge you to write a tribute and read it to your parents, too. Talk together about how you feel about this assignment and about your parents.

Remember whatever you put off until next year is never done - why - because next year never comes.

The Twins: Precious and Princess

Precious and I were born in 1957 and came to England in 1967 at the age of 10.   We came in December, it was cold, and I remember we had coats on. We were told that one of us was running after the car when mum left for England when we were 3 but we cannot recall which one of us did this, probably Princess as she is the younger by a few minutes. The separation was very painful. Mum told us later that she had us when she was around, 20 years old and says that she did not want to leave us.

There are 5 of us, all sisters but one sister lived with my grandmother in Birmingham, and the first time we met her she was laid out in a coffin. We are the eldest born in 1957 followed by our remaining siblings Denise, born 1962, Clarisse, 1969.

We were the only ones born in Barbados.   I supposed they must have decided we were double trouble as we were left behind first with friends of my mother, someone we called auntie but we never knew her name even now.   I am not sure how acceptable that would be nowadays. The memory of this time is vague but there was one situation that I cannot forget. We went with aunt to stay with her relatives, and one of her relatives died. I remember that we were both put in the room of the dead relative to sleep for the night, and we were still very young under 5 and petrified. We probably cried ourselves to sleep, huddled together. That's why we have been so close that where one is the other is, we always followed each other.   That is a big memory of mine in Barbados because of the trauma it caused. There was a big mango tree outside, which I can visualise to this day.

Mother's intention was to come to England for a short period of time.   Most children left behind lived with their grandmother but we never started living with my gran as she was in England. That's probably why we stayed with a number of people before coming to the mother country. At some point the aunt went over with her daughter to England and we went to live with my mother's brother, not sure if it was Uncle Sam and he was married. I don't remember much about it, but I had memories of cornflakes and milk and brushing our teeth with a plant they cut and used to brush our teeth.   It was a happy memory, there was no bad memories. Then our grandmother came back to Jamaica and for a time and it was really great - a happy time. There was lots of going to church, people coming from America and our uncle was there. There were big church conventions. We moved in with Auntie Jane when grandma was sick and she treated us really bad, we were like slaves in the home, and gran was too sick to notice.   The family of our surname were quite rich and the fact that they were not sending us money caused bad blood. We lived at the bottom with aunt and our rich grandmother lived up in a "mansion". At one point we used to visit her house on the hill. I had good memories of our visits. Gran was old, had a hunched back, and gave us Johnny cake, (fried dumpling). The fact that Princess looked like our dad made our aunt treat her worse because from a young age we were told your father was this and that, and that we just weren't wanted. Then gran died. It was a really sad time, people came to stay which was our tradition, and then there was a big long procession in white when gran died from her home to the burial site which was under a tree. Another young cousin came to live with us. When our grandmother died, there was lots of hush hush, lots of closed doors, lots of chicken being killed – obeah, (witchcraft) going on. The people who took gran's land back was said to have done obeah on her because her son was supposed to have taken a land that wasn't his. Nothing changes most of the family squabbles back home remain about land and house. All we saw was this woman, our gran laying in bed absolutely bloated. There were lots of killings and sacrifices and blood being smeared everywhere which was their way of coping. It was a frightening, upsetting and confusing time, and you could not ask questions. Just to fit into society we now just don't think of these things. We learnt later gran died of cancer. Living with aunt was really bad. We remember her sons wetting the bed often and we had to change it. There were no washing machines in those days and we had to do everything by hand. The aunt's husband came back, to make matters worse. We don't remember what he did at the time but we just knew we had to stay out of his way. We were around 9, and we just knew that we could not be on our own with this man. We later discovered that he had tried it on with my mother and my sister, when they were younger so it was clear that he was a serial abuser, but no one spoke about it. His children knew what he was about and we were never sure if they were directly affected.

We couldn't wait to leave as this was not a nice place to be. Mum was in England and realised we were living with this man and sent for us really quickly.

I don't have a memory of my mum before we came here.   Within a year of my gran's death we came up to England.   Precious's last memory of home is getting ready to go to England and being a bit cheeky and saying that she was not cleaning the boys wet bed, and being chased with a stick. Our Aunt took us to the airport and this was the first time we saw the sea, having lived in the country.   It was cold when we arrived. We never recognised our parents but they sent us in pink dresses so they could recognise us when we first arrived. We hated the dresses yet our other sisters liked them. The first time we met our parents I had picked up the wrong case at the airport and got scolded. There were other children on the flight, and having got to know them we wanted to say goodbye to one particular girl and my dad shouted at me Precious, at our first time meeting. Precious felt this thing come down in her and thought this is what it's going to be like, I on the other hand just clung more to my sister.

In those days they would not let children in the house and my mum begged them to let her keep us in the home.

When we came we were traumatised as we cooked, cleaned and looked after the younger two, and could not do any other school activities.   There was no real family time, daddy never really helped, working shifts on the railway and mum was busy doing shifts in the NHS. We just never fitted in after living separately far away during our formative years, so we never really bonded with our parents.

Mum and dad have always fought. My dad treated my mum so bad. When we got to an age we encouraged her to leave which she did a few times until she finally left. It was traumatic. They were often fighting around our dad and the affairs he had that lasted their lifetime together. If it was up to my dad we would not be here, in England, he did not want us to come over. Dad was a disappointment he just never did the things he should do. My dad was very party orientated, he did not get drunk, but women was his thing, and we knew this because they would fight about it. He would give mum twenty pounds for the week and mum would then go to the parties and see the women and demand more money. One of my most horrific memories is dad hitting mum with the foot of the gram, (the old record player). Mum would mash up dad's car than take her pardner money and buy back the car. Nonetheless they were still close and had a very active sex life. Neighbours used to ask "why is your mum smashing up that car." We were scared of our dad so when he came home we either ran to our room or ran to the kitchen to put his dinner on the table. Even though they fought it felt like them against us the twins. They always took each other's side and our younger two sisters Denise and Clarise got to do whatever they wanted but they were young. My first food memory in England is nasty cheese and lettuce. Princess used to wash outside and washed her feet and the English neighbour asked mum why she was washing her feet, but we did this in Jamaica. She remembers getting lettuce and wondered if she was eating bush. Princess looked like her dad so she got the short end of the stick and got beat a lot. They told her - yu face fava, not as a compliment but derogatory, and then mum took out her frustration on me on Precious.

Though we all had the same mother and father we as children we were kept apart. We had it twice as hard. The saddest thing was that our parents weren't able to pull us together as they used to say things to keep us, all the siblings separate. Everything we had we had to get it for ourselves. We know that our childhood shaped our future. Precious used to spend a lot of time looking out of the window not feeling happy. We can't ever remember being hugged by our mum or dad. Now we can say I love you mum and mean it. Mum knew dad from back home from a young age. We understand now that mum could not do without a man - relationship wise and despite his behaviour that's why she never left him, for so many years. I believe she thought she needed a man to do everything like in those days needing a man to buy a house.

We never had any time to have good friends in the early years in England, as we were always cooking, particularly full chicken meals. Princess remembers watching Crossroads when home from school as she had to clean the whole house. However over time Princess made good friends in Lewisham and had a little gang which she was the head of, but it was nothing like the gangs of today, violence was not part of their thing. Precious never did make many friends and remembers not being allowed to travel home via Brixton because of boys and going via Kennington in a route that was just white kids. Eventually we moved to Sutton which was predominantly all white residents. Moving to Sutton was yet another upheaval and the feeling of being ripped away again, it was very painful. We moved often as there was not enough room, and finally to a big house owned by Peabody Trust housing, which everyone thought was ours but it wasn't. The environment we lived in was not pleasant. The twins remember the signs on windows, no Irish, no blacks, no dogs. At 16 when Precious started to work she had to buy her own first clothing and remembers using her money to buy clothes for her youngest sister, Princess who was her baby and I remember doing this with my younger cousin in Barbados who was born in Jamaica but wished she was born here. Princess and the other siblings all went to one school and Precious went to another. This meant me travelling home alone often on my home and getting in the house first. My dad would often be at home because he worked shifts and often arrived shortly after me. I was shocked to feel my dad molesting me one day when we were home alone. I was decorating with my dad and I was up the ladder and dad put his hand up my skirt and touched up my leg. I tried to get out of that situation as quickly as I could but remembered thinking that my dad likes fair women and his young daughter was fair, but very young. I was in secondary school between 12-13 years old and definitely traumatised. We would always think twice about saying anything about anything. There was a time when we would not go anywhere without each other in the house. There were just things you did not talk about. We were not encouraged to have close friends. So I never had any close friends. It was not till I was older that I was able to talk to close friends. I knew she would defend him. I never told anyone for years, far into my adult life, as I was not sure I would be believed or supported.

Amongst all this upheaval my parents' did an act of extraordinary kindness. My mother's younger sisters, went to Canada, leaving our cousins in a children's home, so their dad took one out and rejected one Dominic. Our parents went and got Dominic out. My cousin refers to himself as our brother and will have nothing bad to say about our parents yet he won't talk to his mother who won't tell him who his father is. Our Dad used to pick us up from the nightclub late at night and drop us all home including our friends. It was meant to be embarrassing but it wasn't because he dropped us all home.

I learnt in later years why my dad behaved the way he did. It was a lot to do with his upbringing. He faced rejection at an early age and it continued during his formative years. Our grandad denied my dad was his son, but his grandmother did not and took dad as a very ill sick baby to his dad's family to the posh house on the hill. Dad had felt as though he did not belong anywhere. Born out of wedlock. Placed in the boot of a car. Grandad was a policeman in the district and dad was grandma's only child. Then our gran also looked after one of our sister's who died. Once in the UK we ensured that in the summer every year we went to see gran, dad's mum in Bradford and learnt so much whilst being showered with love.

We then saw our unpleasant aunt who we lived with us in Jamaica in England, and found that she was still mean spirited. 2 of her girls had no children. One son died in Jamaica having been knocked over by a car. Her husband left her to live with someone else but then returned to her when they went back to Barbados. I suppose in hindsight she had a lot to be unhappy about if all she saw was her lifestyle and circumstances. Her husband was a hard man to live with and she had to dealing with this.

Princess decided that before she gives a man the opportunity to treat her like how my dad treated my mum, she preferred to stay alone. Her view was, she didn't need a man. She later believed she cursed herself. Putting up a front that she can cope alone. Her kid's dad started behaving like my dad so he had to go. She could have got married a few times but said no. A white man came to the house and her Aunt Albie run him because she did not believe in mixed marriages. Really she now knows that she has been scared to commit yet now feels ready but realises that so many opportunities have passed her by due to family interference or her fears of being married to someone like her dad. She know it's never too late, and is still living in hope. Aunt Albie was Princess's first home leaving home at 16/17 years and her Aunt Albie was seen as taking sides as it was my dad's aunt. There was a stigma that Princess went there and our mum could not do the job as mum always felt that she was not good enough even though, she was fair and pretty but had a cast eye, that turns up. Aunt Albie's grandson married a white woman in Canada and because that marriage worked she has since come and apologised to me. When she found out my dad was a waster, the big house was not his, she felt sorry for us and changed her behaviour towards us. In 2000 Princess went back to Barbados with my children a very angry woman. 6 years later mum was back in England, and I prayed with her and all of that anger went, so for me my faith has helped me to forgive. Precious is not a Christian so she dealt with it differently and has really just locked the past in her closet called feelings. Princess can go in and out between British and our native tongue, but I Precious couldn't switch I just wanted to fit in, and not be the odd kid that didn't speak the language or like the food - Precious did not want to be picked on. As sisters or even with our parents we could not share how they were making us feel. In addition our parents were too busy fighting and working. So things built up inside us as well as with them. We met our parents at 10 years of age and. Precious got married at aged 20 because this was the only way I could get out. I remembered saying "if it does not work out I can always get a divorce". I felt too cowardly to move out independently. In my time you had to be married to live with someone. Having made this decision I had to live with it and found myself unhappily married, we weren't right together. I think a lot of my experience in this marriage was because I had not grown up yet, but yet I became a mother. I ended thinking my husband has to be completely different from my dad, looks etc. My first husband was Chinese and I have now married a white man. I made a concerted decision not to look at black men. Precious's first marriage lasted 9 years and her second marriage was 22 years.

Reflections on the Twins

Unless you climb the mountain you will never discover what is on the other side

The only way evil can triumph is for good folks to sit down and do nothing

Sibling rivalry is just another form of divide and rule and segregation and separation. In slavery times segregation was on the basis of colour and sex whereas here it took place on basis of age and settlement. In the most basic sense it's all about relationships.

Abuse at home and in the UK

Quote: Dad sleeping around all the time and our parents fighting, but they ganged up against us.

My first thought about the twins was that the first private fostering arrangement they experienced with their aunt neither twin can remember their aunt's name. They were very young but it struck me that a no name aunt, does not give the impression of bonding, warmth and presence. Going from aunt to uncle, then grandmother, and then aunt must have been unsettling with the only common denominator being each other, which is why they are so close. The first aunt leaving them to sleep in a room with a dead person has left a permanent bad memory that does not resurrect memories of warmth, care and love. The good memories resurrected was with the uncle and grandmother, and the good memories related to food. Clearly things that build them up physically but affected and helps the whole body. Things never change, the way to a child's heart is definitely through their stomach. They survived because as the Jamaican saying goes - two heads are better than one.

Lurking in the background throughout this story is the fear of sexual abuse, from any quarters, and thankfully when the twins were with their aunt and uncle prior to travelling to the UK, (even there these things are not spoken of), they knew to keep out of his way. On travelling to the UK they later discovered that their concerns were justified and thankfully left before an opportunity arose. It is good to listen to your conscience. People nowadays are more willing to believe these stories of abuse where children are approached by family members in an inappropriate sexual manner, however there is still the fear associated with breaking up families - if you tell. The shame in this situation, uncle and parent goes deep, the secret remains repulsive, and the betrayal is unacceptable. As the black community is one village, people in our village do know when these things occurred, maybe not straight away but overtime, but these secrets are too painful to be shared until the person is old enough to deal with it or the parents have passed away. Till then they learnt to block it out. Some stories relate to the old tradition fulfilled by those who hold disturbing views and beliefs to: Break dem, (their girl child), before anyone else. In slavery time it was common place for young girls to be abused by the slave masters and were sexually forcibly active from 12 years onwards. The boundaries have only recently since the mid 1900 been enforced, with repercussions for inappropriate behaviour. Thankfully this is now a sad part of our past that remains in the past, but also reflects British history. In developing countries we still see residues of this behaviour in pockets where children are still being married off at 10/11 just before or once they reach puberty.

Looking back during slavery days the majority of families lived separately often in men and women camps to prevent unauthorised, sexual activity as slave masters chose specific men to be mules or studs. These men's roles amongst other chores was to impregnate the women specifically to create more child labour, slaves, and these men would father 30 children and more which was customary in those times but not know his children. Some of the children they had they would not be informed of, so there is already generations of fatherless children who would never have met their dad, either. In addition mums would raise the child until they were 12 and then hand them over to the slave master to begin their lives as child and sex slaves. These children were on birth immediately given the slave owners name because they did not belong to their mother or father but the slavemasters and their role was to raise up future generations of slaves. Children grew up hearing but not knowing who their real parents were. History teaches us that the separation experienced by these children left behind in the Caribbean is an echo of our recent past where children were raised without fathers, and only for a time with mothers. Siblings living separately was the norm and family re-union never started until nearly into the 20th century when families left plantations in search of their partners and children. We became the product of our history. But it does not have to remain this way. History is made on a daily basis.

Sexual promiscuity with fathers is a "throw back" these times and before. This was seen as normal and acceptable, as committing to one person was not productive or economically sensible. Times have changed but there are still many people around now looking for love in all the wrong places and fulfilling their lust. Unfortunately though the economic benefits are gone, the inability to commit can become a habit. The effect on the children is often not realised until adulthood.

Their father's love of fairer women is the desire to date someone that is nearly white as for many years black people were not seen as beautiful and unfortunately black peoples themselves began to believe the lie.   Their dad also experienced discrimination amongst his own which is often the case because he was a darker man. Those memories can affect your adult choices.   It is only recently that media portrayals of black people in the Caribbean have been both red skin and darker ebony men and women. In slavery days the fairer children who were often slave masters illegitimate children received better jobs in the big house rather than work the land. That privilege also came at a cost in terms of sexual abuse towards female and male slaves.

There has always been a thing in our community about – "who you fava?" However this can back fire when the person you "fava" is someone others have concerns about. "Fava" was important as in the early days it was the best way to determine and confirm parentage. But looking at someone, (like the A twin), that resemble a person her father, that is not well liked by some due to his behaviour leads to assumptions being made about twin A's current and future behaviour. In fact they are speaking negative words about the person's future and words can bring unnecessary pain particularly to a child who doesn't understand and cannot choose their looks.

Where did the experience lead them? Both became parents of many children so their children would not grow up alone. The experiences with black men may have resulted in one twin marrying a white man and men of non black complexion, whereas twin A has missed chances of marriage because of past experiences. But it's never too late......

If this accounts reaches into the secret painful thoughts that have never gone away I can suggest possible solutions:

Key 1: Undergo a series of professional counselling to take through any historic concerns that have had a profound effect on your life.

Key 2: If your parents are alive write them a letter expressing how you feel and after giving them time to digest it, contact them to see if they wish to try to bring the matter to a close by discussing previous faults and then forgiving each other. Ask a good friend or family member to attend with you for support if need be

Key 3: If your parents are not alive anymore still write a letter to them expressing how you feel and forgiving them and then burn it as a sign, (symbolic expression) that you have decided to move on

Key 4: If you are creative draw your feelings or write poetry or a song that reflects how you felt and how you are working through the life experiences that you have had

Key 5: Choose to attend group with people that have been through what you have experienced, be it abuse or the trauma of domestic violence in the home but choose to do something.

Remember doing nothing produces nothing—change is an action word

I had a dream...

Reginald the warrior

What was my dad's role? I was not really sure of that, to be honest with you. We never really bonded. I came here around 9-10 years old and had about one year in primary school. School year had already started and I just had to fit in. Dad came to England first and then sent for my mum. I was very small when my parents left me and I can't remember my age. What I do remember is that I was raised by my gran, my grandad had died. My gran was like the matriarch, my mum sister and her kids. It was like a big clan like the Waltons. It was a lot of us and we used to play which took away the pain of mum and dad not being there. Four brothers and sister in my family were left behind, I was the second last so they would have looked after me, but my gran was like a second mum as she raised us. We never called her mum but gran but she raised us so we respected her as the senior person who made decisions. She could comfort you but when we were naughty she would beat us in our sleep because we would runaway but she reminded us that we would need to come home. I remember her fairness as there were loads of us yet we all still ate. I enjoyed home but missed motherly things.

Because of the way we were brought up in a pack you don't miss it as much. We all went to same school and we all had to go church on Sunday and could only not go if something was wrong with us. I can't remember anything about my dad before I came here but my mum's reputation went before her as strict. Mum would write to you and would send things down particularly on special days. Special days at home meant lots of baking, a barrel would come down with loads of clothes which you knew was from your mum. Mum knew her role when she went to England that she still needed to provide for us overseas.

"My dad's role I was not really sure of that, to be honest with you."

I can't remember being sick in any way, but I did hurt myself once. I had the little oil lamps that we should not play with and I went real close and burnt my chest and the scare is still there. I never went to hospital so gran treated it somehow, hospital was not free so we made do.

I used to follow my big brother he used to be my idol and we are still close. Me and my brother came first because I followed my oldest brother everywhere and they then brought the rest over based on sibling friendship. My mum and dad brought all five of us up. I can't remember how we recognised my mum at the airport, straight off BOAC plane, but my brother was older when my parents left so he remembered more. Both parents came to the airport.

My mum is my number one person, my idol. My dad was not that type of person, he never had a dad, does not know how to express himself. Even though you talk to him today. I was scared at first, as I did not know where I was going, new, out of my realm but also exciting like an adventure. I can't remember hugging or anything but I just followed my brother. When we first came all four of us lived in a room, it was hard, no privacy, everything in the one room, bed, paraffin heater. By the time my sister came we had a house, my other brothers came and lived at my aunts. Gradually once we had a house we all came together.

My brother struggled to get and settle into college. Me being younger I was alright at school. I found my dad horrible concerning my brother as I had to share my pocket money with my older brother. He did not show me love, and was not able to bond with us, but clearly had something against my older brother. My dad has never explained. He has never bonded to any of his kids. My dad has a disability and is parallelised from the neck down. His mind seems hard, tarnished and cannot change. He still the same now even though he is paralysed.

None of us every had a father figure e.g. where my dad did something for me, except the regular like put us through school. Even at family events or celebration he would sit in a corner and not participate. If he took us out with him all together it would have to benefit him e.g. wedding. He acted as though he did not want to acknowledge his family. He did not know how to express himself and is closed. Out of all his own siblings he seems to be the only one like that.

I am aware of my dad's other siblings and have met some but cannot engage as my dad has not said that he has family here.

More or less the main family we met was my mother's side. I remember my big brother taking us to dad's mum but within an hour we were heading back to gran, we never had a good experience there, from my dad's side nothing good. She did not have enough space for all of us but there seems to be more to it than that but I never got to the bottom of it.

I went Ernest Bevan School. Then in and out of jobs, sports on a Saturday. Got into little misdemeanors but no serious involvement with police. About 10 years ago I discovered that dad had become unwell. Dad was dragging his foot like he had a stroke and someone noticed it, and he told mum and my sister to mind their own business. People used to see it, dad dragging his feet and then my sister asking him. We were living with him but because we did not have a relationship with him we missed it. He then had a whip lash that resulted in him being paralysed now.

This did not help me because since then I have developed a condition and as its hereditary it would have been nice to ask my dad but he won't talk about it. It has affected my whole life, mobility, living everything. From an active person to a non active person, I am struggling to deal with it but it's good to talk it through to cope and override it. I did not have any children. In my twenties my problem started to affect me and as it progressed I could not concentrate on anything else. I had the operation 2004, went in after Christmas and came out just after April, four months later. The darkest time in my life was then in hospital, not being able to do things for myself.

Had girlfriends but they never turned into anything but my upbringing without that role model had an affect. I am not in a relationship or had children. The nearest I got to parenting is looking after my two sisters and feeling good as they are grown up now. I am in my 50's. I wanted to be a father figure and have a good input and not like my dad, put some good ingredients in them. Only my sister got close to my dad mainly because she saw my dad's mum more than us but me and dad never really connected.

When I was home, life was not bad, but life here has been a roller coaster business, from good schooling to adulthood which was harder because I was not schooled in the life skills. I missed out. If my father had input some of these things into me it would have made me a better man. Dad had been a bus driver and he believed he could do better but he never could and never instilled that in me. The thing is our family came over to work so most of their lives were working, Saturday and Sunday was their day off. Sunday was spent getting ready for work. Never seen us do things as a family which sometimes guides you in how you bring up your own kids. It's only now I see black families learning that we need to be together. When he was in we watched cricket but once he was out we had a good time, more freedom. Dad worked weekends so we could be a family, laugh, joke but when he was there it was a dead family.

Where do you go from here? I don't look too far from here, sometimes there are low points and some better. Hospital not being able to walk was my lowest point, so when I get low I look back at that as my lowest point that helps me see things more positively.

I used to love sports football and tennis and any sport that makes you feel good about yourself and now because I can't do them anymore it like I hate them. It's about retraining my thoughts. When they took something they took a piece of me, that cannot be replaced.

Why my dad is like this is something we don't talk about - so no healing, no resolution.

Moving Forward – Forgiving the Past

Reflections on Reginald

The ultimate measure of a man is not where he stands in moments of comfort and convenience but where he stands at times of challenge and controversy. Martin Luther King

Being left behind with siblings eased the feelings of loss because his mum was not there but his coping mechanism was to treat an older brother as his father figure as he did not have one. You must wonder sometimes if being left behind allowed parent's freedom from their responsibility not just the opportunity to work because once your children arrived it should have been the perfect opportunity to shower them with love.

To live with a father that kept himself away from his children unfortunately showed them that he either did not want them or just cannot show love. Children should be seen and not heard is evident here. Fun was not on the agenda. Some men however are loners and may have never had a loving bond with their parents so cannot show what they do not know. Mothers at that time did not have a voice and accepted even the unacceptable.

Communication really is key to a happy, loving family. As a child he was never sick because the family drank regular herbs, including bitters. Even a severe burn was healed by grandmother using growing things that have healing ability. Now we take pills that contain things that affect our health e.g. side effects to supposedly make us better. Natural really was best but due to poor communication and greed that information is lost. In fact we had to find innovative means of communicating in slavery days using dance and drums but now there is no "crisis", the pursuit of knowledge is less importance, as there is so much of it, and we now go for a quick fix. If Reginald's was more communicative he may have been able to ask about heredity illnesses rather than face a major disability in his young adult life. Natural remedies if at home would have been given but the knowledge of this information is not here. His rejection, from cradle, to adulthood has left deeper rooted scars but whilst his father is still alive it's not too late, to try to build this bridge, it's not a rebuild because the relationship never was, it's a new build. The one thing is certain because his dad is disabled from the neck down, he may refuse to talk but he can't walk away anymore so he can try again another day until........

Remember whatever you put off until next month is never done - why - because next month never comes.

If this account brings tears to your eyes because you remember I can suggest possible solutions:

Key 1: I would use the vehicles available to you to start a conversation with your father particularly if they cannot walk away. Start by playing music they enjoy or looking at pictures that are reminiscent to them. This should open up the door to talk about something in your fathers past that is non threatening to them. Really the aim is to engage your dad in meaningful conversation so that trust is built up and you can really have a discussion about the past and maybe ask questions you have never been able to ask.

Key 2: If this does not work see if you father or mother if the blockage is there would allow you to record some of their history, growing up years and family tree and this would open doors to allow a discussion about who they are and how that has impacted on your relationship now. If they would prefer someone else to record it then go with that also as really you are trying to get them to share using the safest medium for them.

Key 3: If all this fails it maybe that you will need to speak to relative and friends to find out about your heritage particularly if you need information about family illnesses. We do need to bear in mind that illness of old would not necessarily be called the same names that they are known by today, so dig wisely.

Key 4: Finally if you really cannot get a breakthrough enjoy the time you have with your parents, as they latter years are the ones you will remember most so collect good wholesome memories that you can review for a lifetime, take video's, collect pictures and just have fun with them while you can, and leave the past alone.

Moving Forward – Climbing every mountain

History is a funny thing

Black history is a funny thing, not funny ha ha but strange,
Strange because the more you learn, the more that remains hidden,
Black history is a funny thing, not funny ha ha but strange,
Because the more you delve into our past,
The more you find remains.

Some people start from Slavery our most horrific times,
Some people go further back to when we ran our lives,
But wherever your interest lies is where you should begin,
In Africa or the Caribbean or Britain, there is scope within.

My parents came to England, a long time ago,
And left behind a country, a home, a place well known,

To start afresh with children, a job, a home, a new life,
To top it all most men where looking for a beautiful wife.

We set up our own church, they refused tell let us in,
We set up our own social domino clubs, our social hour was big,
We loved to dress with colour, trendy, with much style,
We noticed others followed us, we'd only been here a while.

We came well educated, teachers, nurses, well trained,
They never recognised our gifts, they never saw our intelligent brain,
But manual work was plentiful, so we worked hard to return home,
But it did not take long for us to see, we couldn't afford to go home.

So we lived, we loved, we made mistakes,

and we grew strong,
We integrated into the community, not at
first, but as time went along,
Gradually we became more accepted, inter
marriages began,
But still remained a separate, between us
and most English man.

They had taken down the posters, no dogs,
no Irish, no blacks,
But the sentiments of those words they
never took back,
We moved on, became teachers, solicitors
and the like,
We now have likkle shops, barber shop, even
more rights.

We don't forget our recent past, but we have
chosen to move on,
To create a new history, for our children
coming along,
Today is what we make it, remove the
bitterness of the past,
To grow we must forgive, because we are
Free At Last.

Made in the USA
Charleston, SC
24 October 2015